ICARUS SEES HIS FATHER FLY

JOHN O'DONNELL

DEDALUS

DUBLIN 2004

for Myles
up the gunners

6 · IV · 04

The Dedalus Press
24 The Heath ~ Cypress Downs ~ Dublin 6W
Ireland

Cover Painting: An Fharraige Mór, by Tony O'Malley
(courtesy of Jane O'Malley)

ISBN 1 904556 13 2 (paper)
ISBN 1 904556 14 0 (bound)

Dedalus Press books are represented and distributed —
in the U.S.A. and Canada by **Dufour Editions Ltd.**, P.O. Box 7,
Chester Springs, Pennsylvania 19425 —
in the UK by **Central Books**, 99 Wallis Road, London E9 5LN

The Dedalus Press receives financial assistance from
An Chomhairle Ealaíon, The Arts Council, Ireland.

Printed in Dublin by The Johnswood Press

For my parents

They let me and they watched me.

Seamus Heaney, *Electric Light*

ACKNOWLEDGMENTS

Acknowledgments are due to the editors of the following publications, where some of these poems, or versions of them first appeared:

Acorn, Agenda, Anna Livia FM, Books Ireland, Breaking The Skin, The Cloverdale Anthology Of New Irish Poetry, Cork Literary Review, eAcorn, Forgotten Light, Golden Echoes, The Heart of Kerry, IMJ, The Irish Times, Iron, Out To Lunch, Poetry, Poetry Ireland Review, Poets For The Millennium, Podium, RTE, Seeing The Wood And The Trees, Sunday Tribune, Sunday Independent, Stand, Waterford Review.

"The Majestic" won the SeaCat Irish National Poetry Competition.
"The Loss" won the Bookstop Prize for Poetry.
"Chinese Lantern" won the Irish Times/Anna Livia FM
Poetry Award.
"Icarus Sees His Father Fly" won the Listowel Writers' Week Prize
for Poetry.
"Christmas 1914" won the William Allingham Poetry Award.

Contents

This Child

Icarus Sees His Father Fly

The Majestic

For This Week Only warned the message
in black marker on the latest glossy poster, as we
queued at The Majestic all those rain-filled afternoons
in the summer we discovered sex, and the ravages

of acne. More than the roar and flicker of the screen,
what mattered was what was happening here: wolf-whistles,
the footstamping and cheers from StarCrushed mouths as lights
went down, and we sat through the ads, the jerky newsreel,

Forthcoming Attractions on first dates, row on row
of one-armed crucifixions waiting for the action
to begin. High up, Fitzy — balding, tipsy — knocked back
one more shot as he loaded the projector and shambled down

to stand beside the swing-doors watching over us, a Zeus
in platform shoes. Cloud-eyed, we thanked God for the rain
skittering on streets as we turned, wet-lipped and full of purpose
to each other amid the susurrus of sweet wrappings, urgent

fumblings in the mote-filled dark. We were young and scared
of nothing except heartbreak, the lasso of Fitzy's flashlight
twirling all around us as we struggled with zips and buttons,
groping towards the future with trembling clammy hands.

Where A Poem Comes From

Rowing To America

I face backward to move forward; all I see
is stern, the muscled waves, wake's
disappearing vee. Under, swerve of silver,

fin-surge, stately boom, and under still
the seabed's prehistoric gloom. So long ago
the crowded pier, the reverie that led to where

I'm now, neither there nor here, nothing of me left
except this seat splintering skin, these bloodied oars,
a memory of salt flesh as I haul in the line

again. Nothing. Gulls are watchful gods
as I sea-saw beneath the clouds,
placing my trust in thole and bark

and dip my blades once more, pull up
a meteor shower of flying fish, thumping through
the spume-filled air then plunging back

into the foam — except for one, flipflipping
iridescence at my feet. Ancient scales; the little wings,
sturdy enough to bear a soul. And I devour it. Whole.

Chinese Lantern

The paper harbour twirled in the bulb's heat,
Junks shimmering in the painted Shanghai night.
Over the frame stretched silk was sewn tight,
Appliquéd dragons and pagodas were sweet

Inferences of flurried needles, thread,
Bent heads, blur of finger and thumb
In a sweatshop at the back of some
Boutique or bar, stitching until they bled

Into red bolts of silk. Like flags the Orient
Unfurled in our classrooms at Geography:
The Great Wall. Paddy fields. The muddied Yangtze:
A far-off place we struggled to invent

Is still embroidered ornament. On the shelf
The light is solid, actual; an unco-opted gleam.
Teach me to tell image from pure beam,
To see what shines through instead: the thing itself.

Rhythm Painting
for Tony O'Malley

You heard it first, the lowing skies and roads
still smudges on a palette. Something is moving
under stone-crossed fields,
among the scrawn and scraggle of the hedges;
the breathing, pagan earth. The rain
a robe over the hidden land.
Easel angled to a dowsing stick, you divine this
rite of mud and bog in shade and hue,
hymn the crow-caw scoring the leaden air,
scratches on a canvas.

Elsewhere your brush hovers, landing in eleutherian light.
Each day a blur of distant music; earthlyre wings,
the hum of dreaming seas. Listening, you put on morning
in an impasto of turquoise, reds and blues,
watch moths gather over harvests standing stacked
against the evening; stooks of yellows, ochres, browns.
In the village they are wearing masks and flowers,
voices lilting into night. Ancient cadences,
rituals resonant in your rhythms of paint;
island songs, the occult earth-drummed rain.

The Toolbox

Buried beneath jumble in the attic
a dim gleam: my grandfather's toolbox.
Through dust I trace the legend in a nameplate
on the lid I hardly dare to open
afraid of what is, or is not, inside.
Small compartments stare back, empty,
tidy silences that once held plugs and fuses.
I imagine his hands busy with wires, screwdrivers

making connections. "M.J. O'Donnell,
Oldtown, Co. Limerick." The first electrician
in the parish. That man lit up a whole town
from wobbly ladders, or on his knees
in houses smelling of candle-grease,
a dangling shade and socket in each room.
And always the professional, the teak case
polished, easy by his side. I fumble

in the dark to find him now within
this box he'd carried with him his whole life
that holds him still in dents, scratched surfaces
the grain warm with his fingerprints
light inferences of deft, enviable craft
making lives glow. Outside the evening
brightens to his memory in the street.
I'll touch the wood to feel him touching me.

West of Ireland Teacher
for Sean McSweeney

He works the board once more
By an Atlantic window, explaining
With a flourish, master
Of salt fields and wet light.
In his classroom the children
Have bog-pool eyes and shoreline smiles,
Freckles of bog-cotton, and each lesson
Is a landscape learned by heart.

The Songs

Bird-calls. Hooves of cattle.
Breezes fingering the reeds near water
rivering through moss and stone,
heading for the heart-sigh of the seas
they travelled over, their pockets
stuffed with relics and addresses

and these sounds, shiny seeds waiting to fall
on freshly-opened ground. Some were lost
beneath the highways and the bridges
while others grew roots and survived.
A word put in. Dropped notes. Blooming,
they took new shapes and became

something that is different yet the same,
the voice a father passes to his son.
Blazing heather in a sunset
on the forty-second floor; bodhráns
in the canyons underground.
Curlew-cry the tune night sirens hum.

A Carol

At midnight, the faint sound of a scuffle
High up on icy slates. Fantastic hooves
Wobble, trying to balance in the muffle
Of imagined snow on childhood roofs

Which, if fable, we invented for ourselves
As much as for the faces that peer after:
We thrill to tell of reindeers and of elves
That we may watch small eyes go big, hear laughter

And learn again that what sustains the heart
Is not the proof, but wanting to believe
As we brighten dark days with stories of a start
That still seems improbable, birth on a winter's eve

We sing of tonight, under the starry heaven
Waiting again for the miraculous to happen.

Where A Poem Comes From

The roof that I fell off when I was ten
was at the back of an abandoned house
I'd long been warned against, although

the thrill of loitering there,
deliciously illicit after school
soon wore thin, a drama become casual

until the fall. What made me lose
my footing I don't know; carelessness,
day-dreaming or perhaps

pure chance shaping the drop
that left me on the ground
and roaring, pointing to my shin

at where the rusted hidden spike
had entered in. My eyes filled with
the bloom and ooze of blood at first

but it was the later pain that mattered
more, a deep dull throb that seemed to be
just there, under bedclothes or school trousers,

the new skin forming and reforming as I
kept giving in to the urge to pick at it
again, with finger-nail or pencil-point,

hoping for the cruel vivid slash
so many T.V. baddies wore, but ending up
instead, I don't remember when

with a pale dent the shape
of a small flying fish which made
my class-mates smile. The house

is gone, lines of whitewash
rolled on tarmac, space to park
a hundred cars. And I still have the scar.

Missing Persons

The Last Wolf In Ireland

Before, dark star of eagle; herds of elk
Lumbering through forests, gloom of oak

Hewn since by the acre: shipped to become
The ribs of abbeys and cathedrals, hum

Of parliament. Their fists thumping the benches
Made from wood we'd marked as ours, stain of piss,

As they proclaimed the laws that soon would find us
Gasping in the ditches. Only legends

Left behind: the stolen infant, suckled
Amongst cubs; woolskin covering each pelt

While we moved stealthy through the dozing flock.
No mercy when we needed to attack;

An airy rush, fur tumbling to claw,
Muscle and sinew, our mouths rusting with gore.

Now I paw the undergrowth for carrion, snuffling
Beneath bushes, and watch the soldiers clanking

Into villages. Land being sheared and trimmed;
The new estates. Fire scented on the wind:

A country turned out, turning on its own as
Bounty hunters oil their muskets. Shadows

Over moonlit fields, the locals' silvered faces
Pointing out our sleeping young, the hidden places

They'll name after us when I am also gone
To earth among wing-feathers, antler bone,

The bog dreamtime; in black sod sunk below
Where no shone steel will ever fence or plough.

This Afternoon
Omagh, 15 August 1998

In Lingerie she is fingering a nightdress she might wear,
Her two bridesmaids to-be skitting beside her. Elsewhere

Schoolboys like disgruntled sheep wait in huddles
To be measured up for uniforms, dreaming of girls

And football, a new season this afternoon as summer ends
Diminuendo in the town. Here is a father waiting for his sons,

A baby cooing in her pram, two women browsing for a gift
As shopworkers count the hours down, not long left

Till Saturday night, out for a few jars,
The raised T.V. showing highlights in the bar

Of games played earlier today by scrawny heroes
The whole world at their feet, not much older

Than the two who've just now parked the car, discreet
That in a moment will bring them all together in the street.

Missing Persons

Such heartbreak in each grainy photograph
the family has tearfully supplied.
What intimacy these blurred moments have,

squinting into holiday sunlight
or laughing in the pub before the dance.
We can almost feel the weight

of what has happened as we glance
and then move on, a little guiltily,
past this inference of absence

that already we well know
we'll never miss, just faces
in the supermarket queue

or waiting at the bus-stop for a bus
in the dusk of urban evening,
so long as it isn't one of us

who disappears without ever really leaving
in between the shadows and the light;
an ending we hardly can believe in,

the cluttered bedroom quiet
as police teams drag the rivers
and comb the undergrowth, nothing left

except these souvenirs. Clothes
in wardrobes, ghosts on hangers.
A hairbrush full of hairs.

Bills

She'd hoovered the whole house before the end, every room
left gleaming, spick and span. Polished taps and counters
shone for stricken friends, neighbours who'd drop in

after, to make tea. The funeral arrangements were written out
in her small, still-tidy hand: "Amazing Grace. No flowers."
She'd had the whole event so carefully planned, even to

the final thing she did before she walked across the beach
into the sea: the settling of accounts. Fifty each, the grocer
and the butcher; a fiver in the library for those books

long overdue. At the garden centre the young assistant
beamed: "Well now, Mrs. Mac, I reckon this brings you
right up to date" as he took the twenty, handing her

the daffs. On the table her last words, an envelope
propped up against the vase: "This is no-one's fault.
I just can't go on. I've had enough. My bills are paid."

Showrooms

Arrayed, the latest models here
await your pleasure. Like geishas
they have learned how to forget

tyrekickers, the dent left by each
well-upholstered rump, as the sales
assistant plumps the cushions

once again, brisk wipe of shammy
to restore a faded gleam.
Side by side, the king and queen

sized beds dream of splendour
in a well-appointed room, complete
with walk-in wardrobe and ensuite,

while in the corner a family of three
have high hopes of staying together
now they've been reduced to clear,

the two armchairs proudly flanking
their big strapping settee. But you
know, even as you choose the one

you most desire and give your details,
you too will soon forget the others
that don't match the fabric of your life,

who'll end up being flogged off
to inner city hostels, mottle-stained,
the stuffing almost gone

or the day-room of the nursing home
that's waiting in the suburbs; the T.V.
turned up, blaring on and on.

Conkers

Amongst the scatter of split husks
their new-born shininess persists.
We cupped those polished knuckles
in our hands, scrabbling along paths
under ancient breezy trees to stuff them
into pockets brimming with odd coins, sweet wrappers,
hairy bits of twine. Their muffled clack was
the same sound Cull's beads made when
they swung beneath his robes to kiss the leather
strap, tucked into his belt while he roamed
the yard. Older boys, wily campaigners,
dangled seasoners by the wall, smirking at our frowns
as one by one each new-found world
exploded, fleshy chips arcing to the ground.

Kindertotenlieder

The size three running shoe
beside the railway track.

The nurse shaking her head
under the poster of that team.

The yellow tee-shirt on the washing line.
The short pine box.

The blowing cheeks of the policeman
directing traffic at the scene.

The football sunk in knee-high grass.
The school lined up in uniform.

The cousin who receives a bike.
The mason chipping out the name.

The loosestrife on the river bank
in bloom. The tidy, tidy room.

Lindbergh Reaches Ireland

White knuckles on the joystick
In the frozen cockpit
Half-dreaming of a brightly-lit oblivion.
Tries to hold eyes open with his fingers.
The last sandwich eaten,
Across empty ocean 'Spirit'
Rattles on, towards prayed-for headlands
The Three Sisters greening, and
A fisherman now lets go a wooden oar
To wave up at him astounded, seeing
America in his slipstream
Sky a skein of vapour trails.

Zapruder

His secretary insists: "Mr Z, you just gotta
bring the camera: you might never

get a chance again like this". So he leaves the workroom
where they make the ladies' dresses, 501 on Elm

nearby the Book Depository, collects the Bell & Howell
and walks down to find a place where he'll

see everything, a place where he can get
a real good shot. Past midday now: it's hot

and there's a big crowd gathered here already,
so eager for this moment. "All The Way

With JFK!" The hats and badges. The smiling
sunlit children swizzling little flags, straining

for a glimpse as the cavalcade glides slowly into view
of the sixth floor, Oswald hoisting the Mannlicher-Carcano

and the Governor's wife turns, full of Southern pride
to the movie-star young couple in the seat behind

"You can't say Dallas doesn't love you now!"
the 8 millimeter whirring as Zapruder squints through

the telephoto lens, watching frame by frame
pictures he'll see in his head again, again. Again.

Nearing Distance

I keep your letters bound in red elastic;
no ribbon's silken finery of deceit. Each missive

strives for perfection, refusing irritably the bland, that
sly fifth column of the ordinary. Your rummage

incomplete, this is (you sigh) composed of only second-bests
and write of Paris, rues, the drifting suburbs. I feel

the lace of rain in my face on the Champs Elysées.
Our intimate river's waters darken. Uneased, I

idle over notepaper, replay our favourite record.
The music bustles round me like a housewife

polishing each trace of you. Absence becomes silence.
I busy myself with the address, anticipate a future

correspondence: an envelope tumbling through the letter-box,
perhaps voices crackling over water. The minutes sidle by. In a

house outskirted by the hem of night-fall
you are tending children, drawing them towards bed-time

with a story. Undetected days slip past the clumsy cordon,
hatbrims dipped in an unhurried stroll. Maybe, you say,

we could meet up at Christmas. August is arrested,
the autumn's still curfews the evening. Is this

Suspicion of a subterfuge a sign that we at last are
nearing distance, the amiable dilution of an intimacy? The

rubber band still holds and we have sealed off all banalities, but
it's time which is now ransacking our city, looting in doorways.

Judenbengel

In train-clatter he awakens from a dream
of Mama's strudel, waft of apples warming
in another summer kitchen. Sweet heart of marzipan

and bitter edge he also still can taste, the cake
Hoffman had presented one Sunday afternoon,
new boots gleaming in the doorway as he enquired

for sister Anna. Leaning out the carriage-window
he can see red flags, the skewed black crosses at the centre
fluttering over villages, market squares massing

with uniforms, the bark and clip of drills. Further out
the opened ground, furrows newly turned for vegetables
like those he'd seen in Reinhold's shop. He'd loved

that grocery shop, loved when Reinhold allowed him
help out at weekends. Weighing and parcelling up.
The brisk song of the register until Reinhold yanked him

one day from the window and shoved him back
onto the store-room floor, emptying sackfuls of potatoes
over him, urging he keep quiet. Earthy dark, the tubers

all around him, a thousand silent skulls; Reinhold's twitter
at the counter as Hoffman screeched, demanding to know
where that *Judenbengel* was. Torch-loom: a door closing,

the soldiers stomping off into the street that would be littered
three nights later with the shards of broken windows,
glinting on the ground like fallen stars. Winter creeping in:

into the shut schools and cleared-out houses, frosting the signs
on benches in the park. Baleful trams; the hissing shops.
The evening a girl in ringlets spat in Anna's face Mama opened

the school atlas, a map of Europe on the table while Papy
pulled the smallest suitcase from the wardrobe. "You're
a big boy now" he said. How to choose? Which toy,

which book, which photograph to pack inside
the little case that Mama, Papy must have known
even as they stuffed it full and snapped the catches shut

would hold a life? "But why me and not Anna; why not you?"
"She is older. We will join you soon. Promise you will write."
And he would tell them everything: the border guards, stolid

as Dutch Friesians; clamour of the seagulls at De Hoek as they
boarded the ferry, platoons of children hosting towards England.
Harwich in damp light; the sandwiches they'd chewed

in freezing summer beach huts, name-tagged, waiting
to be chosen: all this he would record in whorls of ink
on paper his house-mother gave him, letters home already

headed for oblivion, another hand stamping the familiar address
'Deported, Auschwitz'. "Promise you will remember us".
As if he could forget the crowded midnight platforms, steam

belching from other trains already loaded for the East, and how
the tears came lumbering down Papy's cheeks, down Anna's
ashen face as he hugged Mama one more time, his own hot splashes

darkening the wool of her last coat, a stain spreading just below
the star she'd recently stitched on.

A Kite Lost In December
for John Shinnors

Here is the sound
Of wind and loss on canvas
Rushing in from sea
Past islands and lighthouses.
Over stubbled fields it comes,
A small high frame of colour
Tugged by unseen string
Towards this abandoned scarecrow town.
Listen: tonight it flutters in the streets,
It knocks against the boarded shops.
It taps for late drinks on the window
Of a pub closed twenty years ago.
The lovers and the children
Are gone, long gone,
Only the cats remain.
Under the bone moon they slink
Around the backs of houses
Beneath lines that wait for empty washing
In gardens that remember snowmen
With carrots for noses
And bright scarves to keep them warm.

Christmas 1914

Dawn. On either side they lean
against each other, shivering
inside greatcoats that don't fit. In
ink-blue air they finger
keepsakes, scribble final letters home
and wait for the command.
And someone sweetly punts
a football into no-man's land.

Who started this? I'd have loved to meet
the man for whom the whole world
was the certainty of stitched leather
at his feet. No notion, surely, of the rights
of smaller nations as he packed it in
among the extra socks and cartridge
belts; all he'd seen then were coats
piled up for goalposts, picking teams,

the usual arguments about
what crossed the line, or didn't
in the end. Now for once the dream
is real as soldiers step from dugouts
and from trenches, wary of this eerie
dress rehearsal until the space is gradually
filled with shouts pluming the air,
frosted ridges crunching underfoot,

the hoofed ball rising high and falling
back, then booted once again into
the middle distance. What is there left
between them except swapped cigarettes,
swigs of vodka and of rum? For hours
after they sit around, learning
new card games, the airs of old sad songs
they still hum as they part, with sheepish hugs

and promises to return. One by one
they disappear, fading into dusk.
Like distant tears the first stars gleam,
as if they know that even after all of this
everything will be different yet the same,
that soon the rats will dart once more
like pickpockets among the dead.
Now evening falls in a swoon

over villages and silent farms that dream
of summer, over the frozen soulless sea,
and over streets in cities on the edge
of history, where boys are still playing
in a dying light, shrieking as they thump
the brand new football plucked
with delighted cries that morning
from under the winking tree.

This Child

And all these things were talked about through all the hill country
of Judea; and all who heard them laid them up in their hearts,
saying "What then will this child be?"
Luke
1, 65-66

i. The Star

Nebula's slow blooming into flame
My birth, a thousand years before that night.
Meteors played dizzy astral games
Beneath Orion as I held high my light
Above caravans of souls, the icy hills,
That dusty kings, far off on raw-kneed camels
Might see where they were headed. Up here
So many others, flaunting their own grandeur
As they jostled in the ether for their turn.
Why I was the one chosen to burn
More brightly than the rest I did not know,
But heard through static murmurings below,
The streets unsettled, new rumours of war
And others wondering what all this was for.

ii.   The Innkeeper's Daughter

Such a look my mother gave my father
When he turned those two away, though he was
Too busy to notice, wondering whether
He'd enough food to go round. Her urgent hiss:

"Go after them; tell them about the shed".
I ran out into the star-chilled evening
And caught them as they plodded up the road.
He was older, grave, but she was young, wincing
As the globe of the child inside her turned.
Across back fields I led them; already beasts
Were in there sleeping, breaths wreathing the fetid
Air. She was close, robes hoicked above her waist
When I went for help. I brought back a rag doll
Later: I suppose I'd hoped it was a girl.

iii.   A Shepherd

I'd had a skinful earlier that night:
We'd all had, and who'd blame us, stuck out here
Freezing our balls off, the wolves and winter
Closing in. Whether that explains the light
I saw, or what I heard next I can't say
But the others saw it too, heard the voice
Telling us not to be afraid, good news
Happening in the town, a baby's cry.
More lights crowding the sky; we got going
Then, running just to get away as far
As we could, till I stumbled near a byre.
Inside, a man distracted, cattle lowing,
A woman's sighs. So strange, and yet so right:
This swaddled child, the star above so bright.

iv. Joseph

Something so actual about a chair;
The honest, sturdy way it holds its ground
Among the off-cuts, shaving-curls. Sound,
Reliable: you know just where you are.
I can use a saw, make sense of wood,
Shape it to a bench, a press, a table,
And up to this, worshipped one true god —
But who wouldn't now have doubts about it all?
First her news before our marriage (the smirks
On neighbours' faces); then, the dreams began.
Along the slow trek south before the birth
I held her close, as if it were my own
Child in there, my life since never the same
As oozing onto straw, dazed, he became.

v Herod And The Children

I know it sounds brutal, even bizarre;
It's not that I'd expect you to understand.
But such unrest; how else could I be sure
One king alone would rule this troubled land?
The business of the star did sound unlikely,
But why else those three would have made the visit
I don't know; as kings themselves, though, surely
They could see the need for order. Was it
Such a crime? It's a smallish town, remember;
So seventy, say — or a hundred, maybe.
And how many would have made it past age two,
Mortality rates being what they were?
No, no bad dreams; I sleep like a baby.
You see, I just did what any man would do.

vi. The Camel Boy

Fine for the three of them, asleep in tents
Or the best rooms in each town that we'd pass through.
Outside we shivered, struggling to soothe
The moans of tethered beasts, and our own sense
Of fear on nights when that high star stared back
At us, reflected in our wide-eyed gaze.
A message came. In the gloomy palace
Staff were nervous, their king sullen, choleric,
Smiling hard as he insisted we return.
Or so the whispers were. By the time we'd come
To the right place one animal was lame:
We unloaded inlaid caskets, brimming urns,
And waited by the fire. The snow still deep
When they came back; I swear I saw one weep.

Icarus Sees His Father Fly

Classics

Like elephants bemused by Alpine snow
we stumbled through histories of Greece and Rome
as Neddie Keane, a Hannibal from Ballina
urged us daily on. We'd chant "mensa",
sit through the grammar and the endless wars,
learning later how to skip off to serve Mass
and afterwards quick nip of altar wine
among soutanes in the sacristy, O sacrament divine.
Ulysses amongst the Lotus-Eaters
had nothing on the nights we spent in Lysters
lined up for the swill, underage but hopeful,
fuzzburned soldiers much too young for battle
until I'd wobble home at closing, tipsy victor,
to find my father in a god-like temper
stalking the house alone, demanding I tell
where on earth I'd been, although he knew full well
and where did I think all of this was going.
And I would try to answer without slurring
but what I meant just came out the wrong way,
the words so jumbled up and hard to say
that I may as well have talked to him in Greek,
more than the beer churning as I'd speak.

Injury Time

A mire, sad posts each Saturday; junior league. Game
Over, home, I'd slump in worship: on the T.V., news
Of how we'd done today. West Ham, a London team;
"The Hammers", we aficionados liked to call
Them. Here was where heartbreak began; the football
Results, age twelve, wondering what they'd done to lose

To that crowd. Your crowd hardly ever seemed to lose
Which didn't make things any easier, each game
Arsenal won one-nil "a victory for football"
You'd trump, as the announcer passed on the grim news.
Voice dropped a semi-tone in sympathy, he'd call
The numbers out that weekly threatened my esteem

For those boys in claret and blue, my chosen team.
But being a fan's about being loyal when they lose,
As well as win; a true vocation, like "The Call"
Priests heard, that we were all afraid we'd hear. The game
Gave us an argot; sendings off, selection news,
Who we're playing next. Back then, only football

Counted, evenings in the garden banging the ball
Again, again against the brick 'til you came home. "Team
Spirit, lads; this is the one — I'm tellin' youse"
Urged 'Woodbine' our nicotine-stained coach, before we'd lose
Once more, our record losing streak of nineteen games
Ended out of pity, a ref's dubious call:

Another match you missed. Seasons later, when you'd call
I'd take up the role I'd learned from playing football;
Defending deep, surprise attack the only game
I knew. I could name each year that East End team
Won the Cup, but can't say when we started to lose
What should have mattered more between us than this news

We exchange instead, our answering machines in use
To record goals by Bergkamp, DiCanio, recall
How, though we'd started well, we still managed to lose.
Home wins, defeats; even the scoreless draws of football
Draw us together now, like some hapless team
One nil down, struggling for a goal to save the game

Knowing we're in injury time; knowing the next call
Could bring the news that it's all over, the ball
Gone dead. Knowing this game's one we can't afford to lose.

Icarus Sees His Father Fly

I've spent hours watching you
Glide, soaring on updrafts
Far above the wrinkled sea

And you nearly seventy!
Up there it's all wind and lift,
Wheeling in the brilliant blue

Harnessed in that brittle frame
Of feather, wood and gum.
You swoop with a delighted screech

And climb again, so high over the beach
You seem closer to the sun
Than me. But it's just one more game

To you, aloft on your own genius
Showing how it's done.
I wonder did you ever doubt

Your own ability, trundling out
Off this cliff edge into the stun
Of that cool rush of nothingness

Beneath your feet? It's unlikely
You stopped first to think of reasons
Why you shouldn't also share the sky

With startled birds, clouds that grumble by;
All confidence, you said. I thought of gravity, some
Shift in the weather; breezes out at sea

Turning into sudden storms instead.
But you're drunk on air now, insistent
That I follow into azure by your side

Making a man of me, or you? So much I've tried
To make you proud. Shouts of encouragement
Loud in my head. Your voice once more. My arms spread.

In The Car

Where are we going today in the car?
The endless I-Spy, stops "to go", and you saying
"All ready?" We seemed to have travelled so far

on those hot sticky seats, rumbling over the tar,
the huge world a blur through the fugged window pane.
Where we were going those days in the car

matters less than time wasted, hour after hour
when we should have been talking. Could we start again?
But already we seem to have travelled so far

apart from each other, the distance a scar
that won't ever heal, that'll always remain
wherever we're going. Today in the car

my son's in the back, pointing out the first star.
"They die before we see the light " you'd explain.
Now red-eyed, I see: to have travelled so far

through the darkness, in silence, wherever we are
— until it's too late; at a graveyard, in rain.
Where we're all going, some day, in a car.
And already we seem to have travelled so far.

Gam-Gam

Not even water with her whiskey — "there's enough in it already" —
on our visits to her parlour, Sundays fingering her piano
while the wireless murmured on. Bullet-proof, my mother said,
two world wars, nine Popes, so when she started getting our names
wrong we just giggled, playing the parts of those other
                                        grandchildren,
oblivious to my father's frown. "They'll never take her out alive"
he shook his head in the car after as we drove back to town, away
from the old gunslinger, whiskery in a twin-set, holed up
                                        in her hideout

waiting for the law — who came immediately, it must be said,
                                        in answer
to her call that all her jewellery had been robbed, the fresh-faced one
bemused to find at last the glistening stones at the back of a high
                                        shelf,
stuffed inside a teapot that she seldom used. In November,
                                        after leaf-fall,
she fell twice. On Christmas Day at dinner her voice shook
                                        a little fist
at my young brother, some imagined slight over the roasties,
                                        turkey breast.
We sulked as birthdays passed, unmarked by cards enclosing fivers:
                                        how
could she forget us, yet remember who had danced with who
                                        on summer nights,

the time the turning of a card had for one man meant the boat, and
so many of their names: the latchikoes and skelpers,

                                go-by-the-walls;
even the runty dog she'd loved, fifteen years dead, whom she still

                                    called
for hours at twilight in her garden while the doctor phoned

                                      my father
to explain. "Thinning of the brain" he said, "there isn't any cure.

                                   You'll need
to keep an eye on her". Which we did, watching as she sailed away,

                                   a liner
in the darkness, the lights on board one by one going out. So that

                                   when
she turned up in her night-dress at the supermarket, where she fell

                                  for the last time,

she was beyond the gaze of neighbours at the checkout, ascending

                                  the ramp
of the ambulance as if it were a scaffold, and beyond us too, the

                                   hurry
of my father to the hospital after they'd told him she was sinking

                                     fast.
Parched flowers. The steel-framed bed. And him, still trying to

                                  work out
what was happening in her head as she turned from some horizon
to ask him who he was, her eldest son: "It's me; it's me, Gam-

                                  Gam",
scaled to a mote in her blank stare, his voice catching at the

                                  moniker
for Grandma our childish tongues once had stumbled on.

Garden

Flowers hummed in their borders. You always loved
The boom and buzz of summer, the swagger of the shrubs
In provident sunlight. Kneeling, ungloved,
Your hands kneaded cool soil. Infant shoots and grubs
Stirred under devoted fingers. Even the sullen mower
Grumbled less, shamed by the spade and hoe
As you urged it over grass on a Sunday afternoon
Your grand-daughter at your elbow, like a bobbing pink balloon.

The night the storm ran riot your head suffused;
Defiled, the garden wept in the profane morning.
In hospital we watch you as a season passes, bruised,
Windfallen. Beside your bed a bead-eyed warning
Screen cheeps at the furrow drilled across your temple. Soon
Handymen will come to clip the aching branches strewn
Over stricken leaves and buds. Someone has sent roses, fresh.
The cellophaned bouquet thuds on the nurses' desk.

Cuff Links

They were my grandfather's,
worn every day along with hair-oil,
white shirts and stiff collars.
The wedding gift she gave, these small
initialled blocks that shone
from that day on, their polished gold
still gleaming as he stood beside the grave.
Afterwards he dressed each day alone,
refusing at the end the nurse's offer,
the clothes as he grew smaller
swimming on him. Fumbling, he recalled
her absence, tugging at the sleeve
so as to bring the cuff-ends near,
in each eyelet a shiny golden tear.

Jigsaws

The slow swing of sun through an early evening;
My uncle hunched at my grandmother's table
Doing jigsaws. Around him the shards of colour gleaming,
Fragments of a broken world. I admired how he was able

To compose again the fractured seas and snows,
Assembling empires from the scattered palaces and cities
Under cool hands. A master. The final piece he'd choose,
Allow me place. For summers those smooth integrities

Sustained me: I grew up in the belief
That the bits would always fit together
And saw him less. Later, red-eyed with grief
He'd shouldered the coffin of my grandmother

With me beside him, taller now, taking the weight.
I watched his face in the bar after as he'd bend
To serve customers, or strain to lift a crate
And thought of puzzles left unfinished in the end

When a couple of the pieces would have disappeared
And seem to matter more for not being here.

The Gift

We shredded Christmas wrapping-paper
to fall whooping on the box, mysteriously
left beneath the tree. Inside, a kite, looking
back up at us like some shy bird of paradise.
The other presents forgotten, we scrambled
for the car, sun glamouring the frosted road
as we passed shiny children parading their
new toys like spoils of war, until we reached

the harbour. The sea flint as we stood;
you paid out the string and on the given
word my younger brother let it go. At first
it was all drag and skitter but then
the wind caught it and it rose; we cheered
and would have watched all day,
admiring as you tugged and steered
until, no warning given, the string

snapped, went lifeless in your hand.
I can still feel the lump and scald of tears
as the kite writhed and fluttered high
over the wave-tops until it disappeared, and
how on the way home when we tried
to hold on to small consolations, imagining
a landing on some foreign shore you
kept driving on, awkward and unnerved by our

dismay but still determined we would learn
how this brief rise before the fall
was inevitable, reciting wind velocities,
the tensile strength of string so we
would understand. Here was something else
you could explain but couldn't fix,
not that different really from when, later on,
you sat by your own father's bed in a ward

that was too hot and smelled of oranges,
your father bemused by all this fuss but still so proud
of his eldest son the doctor as you told him
about the cells growing inside and how it would be
quick and painless in the end. I thought I saw
that man's soul fly up out of his mottled husk,
rising above us as we counted the beads and
murmured prayers at the bedside, but you

accepted only what you found with your own
eyes as you closed his, spatter of wet clay upon
the coffin lid the final sound. Perhaps faith is more
need than belief, the hope of something after
the line breaks, beyond the grief you surely feel
though rarely show in your grim fascination
as you scour newspapers for death-notices
and stand in church for lost companions

who all admired you but sometimes
flinched at how you said exactly
what you thought, the only way you know
a clear-eyed certainty that seems to me
an enviable gift as I write down all this,
trying to find a way of saying things
that faces up to truth, as you do now,
with winter on the streets, no longer

carrying home a boxed surprise of colour
for children who could hardly sleep
so that a vision might rise brightly
in the air above their heads, but waiting
instead for what you see as your own
end, your last descent to earth a fall
out of the sky into the ocean
full of drowned kites far below.

The Loss

You are everywhere I look about this house
Hiding under chairs or around doorways,
Longed for like a small chance missed

Imagined yet. Giggles from an empty corner;
That bump behind the drapes a wind
Gusting through a broken pane. This is

The still life of your absence, etched
In silence. Ashes in the grate are unsung names
For you; the bowed heads of flowers

Bright bedroom colours I'll unpick
From a vase in the bay window
That today is framing swollen hills and

Clotted darkening streams, the winter
You leave after, a shadow gone through
A gap in the fence only a child could fill.

Delivery Room

The ultimate sleight of hand, those white gloves,
Fingers all business when the time arrives
To pluck as from a conjurer's sleek hat
Another of ourselves. What's a poet at
In here, in halo-light, beside the heart
-stopping machines? No dark indulgent art
Preening itself above a field of snow
Could render more visceral or more raw
This moment, me clinging on for dear life
To the rails; and you, voice rising as if
This too were rapture, urged and urging on
What comes now into the room, as we strain
To hear the sound we've held our breath to share —
That prelapsarian squall, filling the air.

Butterflies

This evening, nothing unusual
About this bed-time ritual
Nothing cleaner or more palpable

Than your delighted shrieks and splashes
As you hammer bath-water, all purpose
Or pour cupfuls over upturned toys,

Submerged, helpless. Later you burrow
In the bedclothes, wood creature before winter
While darkness gathers at the window.

The door's pulled to; one last sly creak.
Thieves in our own house, we speak
In whispers, creep upstairs once more to check

On you, then fall asleep until your sudden cry
Hauls us from bed in the small hours, and we
Come trudging, slightly stunned, the way

Others in another time went, herded onto trains
Their children immaculate, holding hands
Wild eyed, afraid of where the line would end:

Concrete and wire. Watchtowers. Each day
They filed into the yard, silently
Gaunt rumours of death. *Arbeit macht frei*

The soldiers said, free as the butterfly
That once, just once, a young boy
Saw flit over the fence from fields nearby,

Grace-note from a loved remembered tune
Jinking about him in the dizzying sun.
Then, a soul rising, the butterfly was gone

Disappearing into hazy distance
Like childhood memories. Innocence.
That boy is dead long since

But you are here, cherished and suckling
On a bottle. Outside the world is waiting
To bring on another summer morning,

Birds fussing in the trees.
Soon the sky will fill with butterflies,
Their wings dappling the air, ease

And flutter, lilt of a child's song
That breaks the heart in two and then is gone.

The Match
in memoriam J.F.
for Paddy

The doors and boot banged shut, the engine not
yet started and you'd be switching on. "He hits it
long again"; how many Sundays did we hear
a high ball arcing through a summer sky before

being plucked out and belted back into the maw
of our car, among chocolate stains and crisps, more
toothsome fizz-filled drinks than we could finish?
"A right shemozzle here", O'Hehir in the Yiddish

screeching with excitement, my young brother and I
trading pinch for pinch in the back seat as we
headed for the shore, hoping the rain would finally get bored
with us, drift off to ruin someone else's day. You'd

always drive, though you were nowhere near
the spattered windscreen. Eyes fixed in a beatific stare
beyond Strand Road, the seagulls hanging round like knives;
all you could see were goals and points and wides,

Micheál's frenzied commentary yammering non-stop
from the speaker. Even when you'd park you'd keep
the spell, carrying a transistor over still-damp sand,
a tabernacle tuned in to Athlone, the same one I'd

collected after from the hospital, with the rest of your things.
I'm turning the dial now, following the wave-bands
in case I'd find you. But the only sound I hear is the soft hiss
of the sea. In the end you bowed your head, the way you'd always

done at Mass, but on those Sunday afternoons gave thanks and
praise for hurling and football; me a sherpa stumbling behind,
lugging bathtowels and a deckchair as you strode ahead to join
the congregation, stretched out beside battered radios along

the beach or in the dunes until "The final whistle", tinny cheers
of far-off crowds rising above us like hosannas in the air.

Sea Language

I was seven when you first taught me
The language. Halyards. The mast.
Mainsheet. Boom. You'd hoist
Those words above us, proudly,

As if you'd made them
Specially for me. Our house
Was a ship full of sails and shouts,
The rattle of rigging, and you at the helm,

A voice that was always there
Even after gales and waves had died.
I can still hear you inside
A harbour bar, ashore somewhere,

Talking up a storm while I
Shivered and drank Cokes until I almost burst.
Now, beerbellied, I can taste
The salt you left, and keep a weather eye

The way old sailors do.
Our lives together have been distances,
Arguments over routes, directions,
Which way the wind really blew;

The usual son and father stuff.
These days I prefer squalls to the silences
In the wary talk of sea between us,
Afraid of when our craft won't be enough.

The Grip

Later, on a summer's evening, we drive out
to my father's club to play. "It's time you took up
golf " he says, meaning that it's time I spent
less time in the pub. We park among the sleeping

chrome and head for the first tee. Swathes of green
and figures clustered everywhere, but all I can see
is my father as he steps up to plant the ball: a pause
and then he hits off neatly; short, but straight and true.

My turn. I draw a sword from the borrowed bag
and wait. "The club is an extension of yourself"
he reminds. I feel the five-iron go limp in my hands.
"Don't try to hit too far too soon". I am going to show

him and the watching world; I am going to smash
this ball onto the moon. Blood-thunder; the club-head
hurtles past. I gaze hopefully a hundred yards ahead
then back down at my feet: the ball, unmoved, still there.

This is called "a fresh air". Another go; the ball squirts
twenty yards out left. Already I am struggling to keep up
with him, listening to the same advice I seem to have
been hearing all my life: *Take it easy*. Instead of getting

closer I am further away than ever, slashing and
hacking through scutch grass, or looking for a ball
I'll never find in the deep rough: in trouble everywhere.
Keep your head down. He's out on the fairway,

alone; I can hear the small clean thwock as he swings
and follows through, the same thing every time,
mechanical, unrelenting like the arguments
we have each time we meet. Hummed snatches

of Sinatra as he waits for me to join him, so distant still.
Go back slowly. I am counting once again the atrocities
of our wars, the years of peace that might have been
now lost to us as surely as those dimpled spheres

long forgotten, nesting in the gorse. The light fading,
he turns to me: *Let's finish here.* He bids me come
out from the weeds and thorns and I do, ending up
beside him on the edge. He plops a new ball

down, then steps behind and puts his arms round me.
I feel his hands closing over mine. *Try holding it*
like this. The club purrs, lofts the ball into the dusk.
So close then, the two of us; almost close enough to kiss.

The Dedalus Press

Icarus Sees his Father Fly

John O'Donnell